DISCOVERING THE UNITED STATES

Vermont

BY CHRISTY MIHALY

Kids Core

An Imprint of Abdo Publishing
abdobooks.com

abdobooks.com

Published by Abdo Publishing, a division of ABDO, PO Box 398166, Minneapolis, Minnesota 55439. Copyright © 2025 by Abdo Consulting Group, Inc. International copyrights reserved in all countries. No part of this book may be reproduced in any form without written permission from the publisher. Kids Core™ is a trademark and logo of Abdo Publishing.

Printed in the United States of America, North Mankato, Minnesota.
052024
092024

Cover Photo: Shutterstock Images
Interior Photos: Shutterstock Images, 4–5, 7 (top left), 7 (bottom left), 8; iStockphoto, 7 (top right), 24; Carol Skelcher/Alamy, 7 (bottom right); Toby Talbot/AP Images, 10–11; Viktor Cvetkovic/iStockphoto, 13; Carol M. Highsmith/Buyenlarge/Archive Photos/Getty Images, 15; Robert Nickelsberg/Getty Images News/Getty Images, 16; Justin Cash/Photodisc/Getty Images, 18; Sean Pavone/Shutterstock Images, 20–21; Kumar Sriskandan/Alamy, 23; Gabe Shakour/Shutterstock Images, 25; David Lyons/Alamy, 26; Red Line Editorial, 28 (top), 29 (left); Felix Lipov/Shutterstock Images, 28 (bottom); Ron and Patty Thomas/iStockphoto, 29 (right)

Editor: Christa Kelly
Series Designer: Katharine Hale

Library of Congress Control Number: 2023949374

Publisher's Cataloging-in-Publication Data

Names: Mihaly, Christy, author.
Title: Vermont / by Christy Mihaly
Description: Minneapolis, Minnesota: Abdo Publishing, 2025 | Series: Discovering the United States | Includes online resources and index.
Identifiers: ISBN 9781098294168 (lib. bdg.) | ISBN 9798384913436 (ebook)
Subjects: LCSH: U.S. states--Juvenile literature. | Vermont--History--Juvenile literature. | Northeastern States--Juvenile literature. | Physical geography--United States--Juvenile literature.
Classification: DDC 973--dc23

All population data taken from:
"Estimates of Population by Sex, Race, and Hispanic Origin: April 1, 2020 to July 1, 2022." *US Census Bureau, Population Division*, June 2023, census.gov.

CONTENTS

CHAPTER 1
The Green Mountain State 4

CHAPTER 2
The People of Vermont 10

CHAPTER 3
Places in Vermont 20

State Map 28
Glossary 30
Online Resources 31
Learn More 31
Index 32
About the Author 32

About 3 million people visit the Appalachian Trail each year.

CHAPTER 1

The Green Mountain State

In July 1900, Benton MacKaye stood on the peak of Stratton Mountain in Vermont. He gazed out over the mountains. He felt like he was on top of the world.

Few people got to see this view. There weren't many paths into the Green Mountains.

MacKaye and his friends had walked through farms and thick forests to get to the mountain.

Suddenly, MacKaye had an idea. People could make a trail along the mountains. His dream came true in 1937 when the Appalachian Trail was completed. Today, it stretches from Georgia to Maine. Vermont holds about 100 miles (161 km) of the beautiful trail.

Vermont's Land

Vermont is in the Northeast region of the United States. Canada is to Vermont's north. New Hampshire is to the east. Massachusetts is to the south. New York is to the west.

Vermont has many mountains and forests. Forests cover more than 75 percent of the state.

Vermont Facts

DATE OF STATEHOOD
March 4, 1791

CAPITAL
Montpelier

POPULATION
647,064

AREA
9,616 square miles
(24,905 sq km)

STATE BIRD
Hermit thrush

STATE TREE
Sugar maple

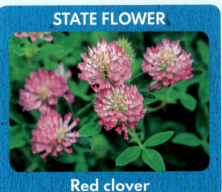
STATE FLOWER
Red clover

STATE ANIMAL
Morgan horse

Each US state has a different population, size, and capital city. States also have state symbols.

Moose, black bears, and other animals live in these woods.

Vermont also has many rivers and lakes. The Connecticut River flows along Vermont's eastern border. It stretches 410 miles (660 km).

Lake Champlain has borders with Vermont, New York, and Canada.

Lake Champlain, the state's biggest lake, is on the western border. The lake is about 120 miles (190 km) long. Many animals depend on these waters, including beavers, ospreys, and trout.

Mud Season

People who live in Vermont often say they have five seasons. The fifth season is mud season. It lasts from April to June. That is when the snow melts and mixes with dirt. During mud season, there is mud everywhere.

Climate

Vermont has cold and snowy winters. On average, it gets more snow than any other state in the country. Springs are often rainy. Summers are warm.

Vermont is famous for its fall colors. The state's maple trees make autumn especially beautiful. The leaves turn red, orange, and gold.

Further Evidence

Look at the website below. Does it give any new evidence to support Chapter One?

Vermont

abdocorelibrary.com/discovering-vermont

The word *Abenaki* means "People of the Dawnland."

10

The People of Vermont

American Indians have lived in Vermont for more than 10,000 years. The state was first home to the Abenaki and Mohican nations. They hunted, gathered, and farmed. There are four state-recognized American Indian nations in Vermont today.

Samuel de Champlain entered Vermont in 1609. He was a French explorer. Champlain traveled with a group of American Indians.

More French people arrived in Vermont later in the 1600s. English **settlers** followed in the 1700s. They built forts, farms, and towns. They forced American Indians to leave their homes.

The Republic of Vermont

Vermont fought in the Revolutionary War (1775–1783). During the war, thirteen of Great Britain's North American **colonies** fought Britain. They wanted to form their own country. Vermont fought against Britain too, but not as a colony. In 1777, Vermont became its own separate country. It was called the Republic of Vermont.

Vermont's current flag was chosen in 1923.

The Americans won the war. They formed the United States. Vermont eventually asked to join the country. New York objected. It wanted Vermont's land. Finally, in 1791, Vermont became the fourteenth state.

Vermont Today

Today, about 647,000 people live in Vermont. Most of these people aren't clustered in big cities. Almost two-thirds of people in Vermont live in small towns.

Almost 92 percent of people in Vermont are white. About 2 percent are Hispanic or Latino. Another 2 percent are Asian. Approximately 1.5 percent of people are Black, and 0.4 percent are American Indian.

Industries

Many people in Vermont work as farmers. They grow apples and sweet corn. Some produce maple syrup. Other farmers raise cows for milk.

Maple syrup is made by collecting and boiling maple tree sap.

Some Vermont residents have jobs collecting and selling the state's **natural resources**. One such resource is granite. Granite is a hard stone used to make statues and buildings.

Vermont's lumber industry supports 20,000 jobs.

Wood is another important natural resource in Vermont. Foresters cut down trees to get **lumber**. Lumber is used to make furniture and houses.

Tourism is also an important **industry** in Vermont. Tourists visit year-round. Many people in Vermont work as tour guides or as service workers to take care of the visitors.

Culture

Outdoor activities are important in Vermont. Many people in the state enjoy hiking and biking.

No Billboards

In 1968, Vermont banned roadside billboards. The state posts plain signs with information for travelers. But large advertising signs are not allowed. Vermont lawmakers believe people want to see the state's beautiful scenery, not giant signs.

Snowshoes allow people to hike in winter without sinking into the snow.

In the winter, residents spend time skiing and snowshoeing.

Food is another important part of Vermont's culture. Each season brings new local foods. Apples ripen in late summer and fall. That is when people make cider and apple pie. In spring, people eat native ferns called fiddleheads. And many Vermont treats are flavored with maple syrup.

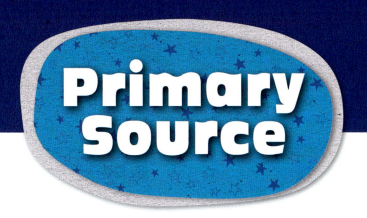

Jenna Baird is a farmer in Vermont. She talked about her mission:

> We believe that when you eat good food, you connect to the land. Our mission is to help you do that.

Source: "Meet Jenna Baird—The 2022 Fantastic Farmer!" *State of Vermont: Agency of Agriculture Food and Markets*, n.d., agriculture.vermont.gov. Accessed 5 Oct. 2023.

Point of View

What is the author's point of view about farming? What is your point of view? Write a short essay about how they are similar and different.

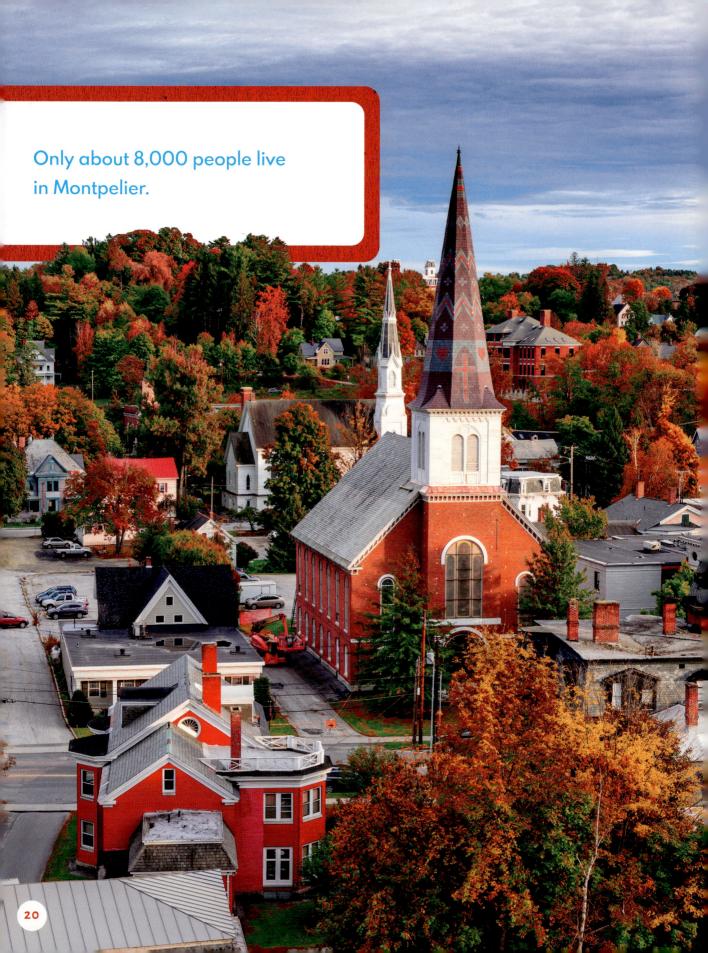

Only about 8,000 people live in Montpelier.

CHAPTER 3

Places in Vermont

Vermont's capital is Montpelier. The city is located in central Vermont. It is the least **populated** state capital in the country. Montpelier is home to the Bragg Farm Sugar House. The farm produces maple syrup. People can tour the farm.

21

Burlington is Vermont's most populated city. It is on the shore of Lake Champlain. The city has several art museums for visitors to explore.

Parks

Marsh-Billings-Rockefeller is Vermont's only National Historical Park. The park is named after three famous **conservationists** who lived

Lake Monster

The Abenaki believed a monster lived in Lake Champlain. The legend spread as more people came to Vermont. Many people have reported seeing a mysterious, dinosaur-like creature in the water. Today, the monster is a popular legend among locals. People in Vermont fondly call the monster Champ.

Visitors can tour a mansion that belonged to the conservationists who used to live in Marsh-Billings-Rockefeller National Historical Park.

on the land. Visitors can learn about how the conservationists protected their land. People can also explore the park's winding trails.

In Abenaki stories, a giant hero named Gluskabe uses Camel's Hump as a seat.

Vermont has 55 state parks. The largest is Camel's Hump State Park. The park is home to Camel's Hump, one of Vermont's highest mountains. Hikers can climb to the mountain's peak.

Quechee Gorge State Park is named for Quechee Gorge, a narrow river **valley** with steep rock walls. Visitors can camp in the park and hike in the gorge. Some people enjoy kayaking the river that flows through the gorge.

The Quechee Gorge is more than 1 mile (1.6 km) long.

Landmarks

Vermont has many historical landmarks. One is Shelburne Farms. The farm was founded in the 1800s. It is still a working farm. Visitors can learn about food and farming.

Vermont's Morgan Horse Farm is home to more than 40 Morgan horses.

At the Morgan Horse Farm, people breed and raise Morgan horses. This strong, fast breed of horses was first bred in Vermont.

The farm has been a horse breeding facility since 1907. Today, the University of Vermont runs the Morgan Horse Farm. Visitors to the farm can see the horses and learn about the breed.

Whether people enjoy farms or mountains, there is plenty to see in Vermont. People can learn about the state's fascinating history, try local foods, and enjoy nature all year round. The Green Mountain State is a special place.

Explore Online

Visit the website below. Does it give information about Morgan horses that isn't in Chapter Three?

Morgan Horses

abdocorelibrary.com/discovering-vermont

State Map

KEY
 Capital Park
 City or town 📍 Point of interest

Mount Mansfield

28

Vermont: The Green Mountain State

Underhill State Park

Glossary

colony
an area that is controlled by another country

conservationists
people who protect the environment

industry
a group of businesses that serve similar purposes

lumber
logs used as building material

natural resource
a material found in nature that can be used by people

populated
settled or lived in

settlers
people who moved to a new area

valley
a low area of land

Online Resources

To learn more about Vermont, visit our free resource websites below.

Visit **abdocorelibrary.com** or scan this QR code for free Common Core resources for teachers and students, including vetted activities, multimedia, and booklinks, for deeper subject comprehension.

Visit **abdobooklinks.com** or scan this QR code for free additional online weblinks for further learning. These links are routinely monitored and updated to provide the most current information available.

Learn More

Berne, Emma Carlson. *The History of the American Revolution.* Rockridge, 2021.

Mazzarella, Kerri. *Morgan.* Crabtree, 2024.

Tieck, Sarah. *Vermont.* Abdo, 2020.

Index

Abenaki Nation, 11, 22
Appalachian Trail, 6

Burlington, 22

Camel's Hump State Park, 24
Connecticut River, 7

de Champlain, Samuel, 12

Lake Champlain, 8, 22

MacKaye, Benton, 5–6
Marsh-Billings-Rockefeller National Historical Park, 22–23
Mohican Nation, 11
Montpelier, 7, 21
Morgan Horse Farm, 26–27

Quechee Gorge, 24

Revolutionary War, 12

Shelburne Farms, 25
Stratton Mountain, 5

About the Author

Christy Mihaly has lived in Vermont for 20 years. She is a children's poet and author and has written more than 35 books, mostly nonfiction. She loves paddling Vermont's waters and exploring its forests through all five of the state's seasons.